How To Draw

Cartoon Characters

by Renzo Barto

Watermill Press

Library of Congress Cataloging-in-Publication Data

Barto, Renzo.
     How to draw cartoon characters / by Renzo Barto.
        p.   cm.
     Summary: Instructions for drawing a variety of human figures and
animals in cartoon style, accompanied by black and white line
drawings.
     ISBN 0-8167-3265-5 (lib. bdg.)   ISBN 0-8167-3218-3 (pbk.)
     1. Cartoon characters in art—Juvenile literature.   2. Drawing—
Technique—Juvenile literature.   [1. Cartoons and comics.
2. Cartooning—Technique.   3. Drawing—Technique.]   I. Title.
NC825.C37B37   1994
741.2'6—dc20   93-23057

Materials

Here's what you need to draw all kinds of cartoon characters:
    medium pencil (#2)
    fine- to medium-point black felt-tip marker
    eraser
    8 ½" x 11" (21.5 cm x 28 cm) sheets of white paper
    tracing paper

Use the tracing paper to copy the drawings in this book. It will give you a good idea of sizes, shapes, and proportions to use.

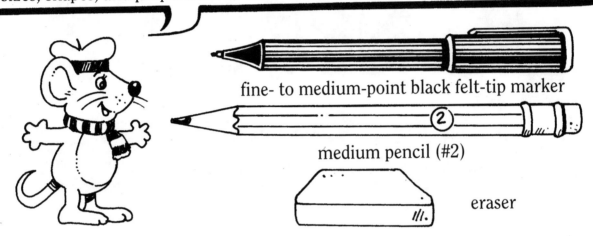

fine- to medium-point black felt-tip marker

medium pencil (#2)

eraser

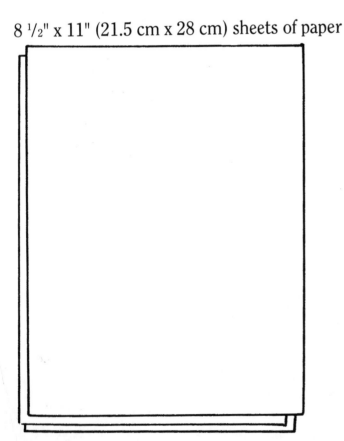

8 ½" x 11" (21.5 cm x 28 cm) sheets of paper

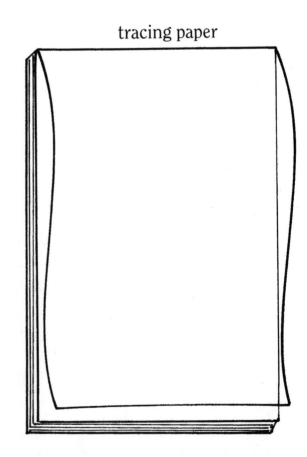

tracing paper

square   circle   rectangle

oval   triangle

1 Start with the shapes that work best for your design.

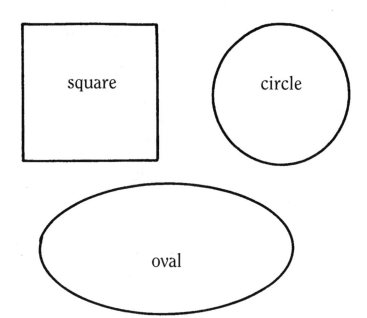

Basic Shapes

Here are the basic shapes you can use to draw everything in this book.

Start by drawing the first steps lightly in pencil. Then connect the shapes, and add details like the eyes, nose, and so on. Then make the lines softer or sharper, depending on the effect you want. Next, use the marker to outline only the lines you want in your final drawing. Fill in the areas you want to highlight. When you're finished, erase any leftover pencil lines.

2 Adjust pencil lines to make smoother shapes. Indicate where the eyes and nose should be.

3 Complete the eyes and nose using your marker. Outline the shapes you want to keep. Then erase all pencil lines.

Clowns

1 Use a pencil and some of the basic shapes to draw the outline. To make the umbrella, draw a half-circle, then draw a line for the handle.

2 Connect the basic shapes and smooth out lines. Add an eye, mouth, and suspenders. Draw fingers on the hands, and make the bottom edge of the umbrella wavy.

3 Use your black felt-tip marker to outline the lines you want to keep in your final drawing. Add highlights like polka dots, socks, and shoelaces. Erase all unwanted pencil lines.

1 Draw the outline using the basic shapes. Draw a circle for the balloon and a line for the string.

2 Connect the basic shapes and smooth out lines. Add eyes and add details to the collar. Draw the clown's suit and add polka dots. Draw fingers on his hand.

3 Outline the lines you want to keep with your felt-tip marker. Fill in fun details like curly hair, shoelaces, mouth, eyebrows, and a design on the clown's hat and suit. Erase all pencil lines.

Sports

1 Start by lightly drawing the basic shapes.

2 Connect the basic shapes and smooth out lines. Draw fingers on the hands and cleats on the bottoms of the shoes.

3 Use your felt-tip marker to add details to the face, shoes, helmet, and shirt. Add details to the football. Erase unwanted pencil lines.

1 Begin by drawing the basic shapes. Add a small curve under the pitcher's right foot for the pitcher's mound.

2 Connect and smooth out the basic shapes. Sketch in details on the glove, baseball, and the pitcher's eye. Add hair.

1 Draw the basic shapes lightly in pencil. Draw a circle for the basketball.

2 Connect the shapes and smooth rough edges. Add hair, nose, fingers, and socks to your drawing.

3 Add highlights to the basketball and your player with the felt-tip marker. Add eyes. Be sure to erase unwanted pencil lines.

3 Outline the pencil lines you want to keep with your felt-tip marker. Add more detail to the pitcher's face, shoes, and shirt. Erase pencil lines.

7

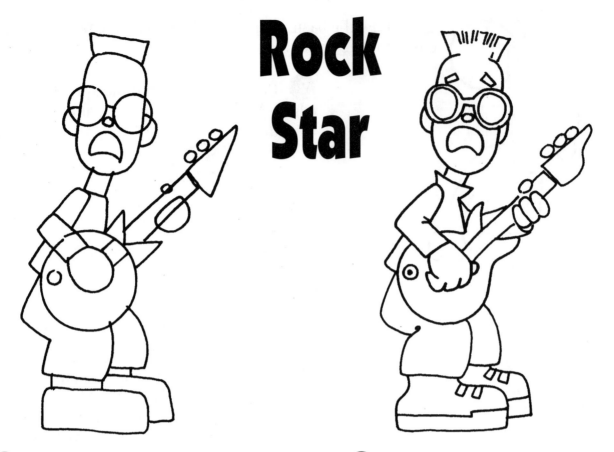

Rock Star

1 Lightly draw the basic shapes.

2 Define the basic shapes by connecting the lines and smoothing them out. Add details to the hair, face, guitar, and sneakers.

3 Use your felt-tip marker to go over the pencil lines you want to keep, and to add final details. Add an amplifier to make the rock star really rock! Erase unwanted pencil lines.

Genie

1 Help this genie come out of his lamp! Begin by drawing the basic shapes lightly in pencil.

2 Complete the shape by connecting the lines and rounding them off. Add details to the genie's face, hands, and hat. Draw the vest and sash.

3 Complete your drawing by adding highlights with your felt-tip pen. Draw a design on the genie's lamp, and add accent lines around his body to make it seem like he's moving. Erase pencil lines.

King

1 Draw the basic shapes lightly in pencil. Draw a circle and a straight line for the king's rod.

2 Connect and round the shapes. Draw the king's coat, vest, and pants. Add details to his crown and face.

3 Use your felt-tip pen to add final highlights. Add fur trim to the king's coat. Go over all the pencil lines you wish to keep, and erase unwanted lines.

Queen

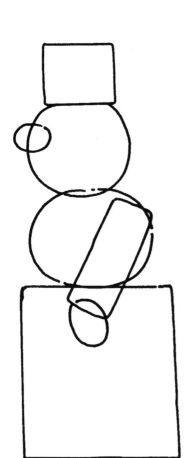

1 Start by drawing the basic shapes.

2 Smooth out lines to create the dress and crown. Add details to the face, crown, and dress. Draw fingers on the hand and make the bottom of the queen's dress wavy.

3 Add the mouth and more details to the crown and dress with your felt-tip marker. Go over pencil lines you want to keep and erase all others.

11

Magician

1 Help the magician pull the rabbit out of his hat! Draw the basic shapes lightly in pencil. Draw ovals for the rabbit's ears.

2 Use your pencil to sketch the magician's hair, mustache, mouth, and suit details. Add eyes and a mouth to the rabbit.

3 Outline the pencil lines you want to keep with your felt-tip marker. Add final highlights to the magician's pants, shoes, and hat. Erase pencil lines.

Astronaut

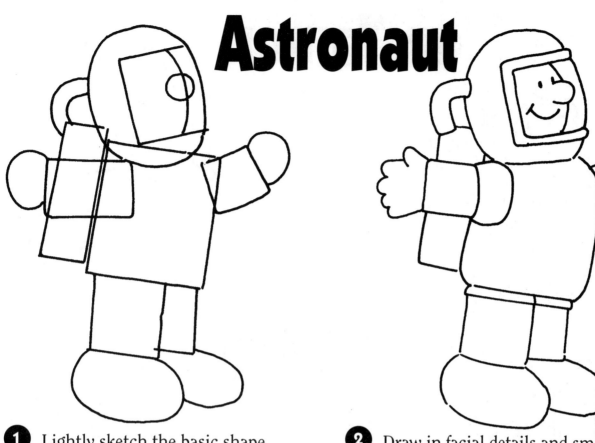

1 Lightly sketch the basic shape guidelines. Draw a curved line and an oval for the astronaut's face.

2 Draw in facial details and smooth out lines. Add fingers to hands.

3 Use your black marker to add final highlights. Draw a picture of the moon's surface - don't forget to add craters and moon rocks. Erase unwanted pencil lines.

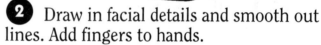

Lion Tamer

1 Using the basic shapes, draw the guidelines for the lion tamer. Add a curved line for his whip.

2 Sketch in details and smooth rough lines. Add a feather on the front of the hat.

3 Trace over pencil lines you wish to keep with your felt-tip marker. Fill in the boots, and highlight other areas. Erase pencil lines.

14

Ringmaster

1 Begin by drawing the basic shapes. Draw two triangles and a small circle for the bow tie.

2 Connect the basic shapes and smooth rough edges. Draw eyes and mouth. Add fingers to the hands, and sketch the coat, vest, and pants.

3 Use your felt-tip marker to draw in hair, eyebrows, and a mustache. Fill in the bow tie, and add highlights to the hat. Go over the pencil lines you want to keep, and erase unwanted lines.

Mad Scientist

1 Lightly sketch the basic shapes.

2 Smooth rough edges. Add hair, eye, and mouth details. Draw fingers on the hands.

3 Draw a fun pattern on the pants with your felt-tip marker. Add a bow tie and mustache. Fill the beaker with liquid. Erase unwanted pencil lines.

Painter

1 Draw the basic shapes. Draw a square above the hand for the paintbrush.

2 Connect the basic shapes and smooth them out. Sketch in hair, eye, and mouth. Add fingers to hand. Draw details of paint bucket.

3 Use your felt-tip marker to go over any pencil lines you wish to keep. Draw a polka-dot design in the paint can, on the wall, and on the paintbrush. Add details to the painter's hat and shirt. Erase unwanted lines.

Sea Captain

1 Sketch the outline of the captain and the wheel using the basic shapes.

2 Connect the shapes and round off the hard edges. Begin sketching in details on the hat, face, coat, and pants. Draw in the captain's hair.

3 Add final details and highlights with your felt-tip marker. Go over all the pencil lines you wish to keep and erase all others.

Pirate

1 Sketch the pirate's outline using the basic shapes. Draw one large and two small rectangles between the hands for the concertina.

2 Add toes to the feet and fingers to the hands. Add facial details and a design on the bandanna. Refine the concertina, making the lines on the large rectangle wavy.

3 Draw stripes on the pirate's shirt with your felt-tip marker. Add a beard and hair peeking out from under the bandanna. Draw in final highlights and trace over pencil lines you want to keep. Add some musical notes and accent lines and you can almost hear the music! Erase unwanted pencil lines.

19

Cowboy

1 Lightly pencil in the guidelines using the basic shapes. Don't forget the hat!

2 Connect the basic shapes and smooth the edges. Shape the hat and boots. Add detail to the face. Sketch a vest, gun, and holster. Add fingers to the hand.

3 Draw the mouth with your felt-tip marker. You can add a design to the bandanna around the cowboy's neck. Add eyebrows and final highlights to your drawing. Go over pencil lines you want to keep, and erase all others.

Letter Carrier

1 Begin by drawing the basic shapes. Put a rectangle in the right hand.

2 Start filling in details. Refine the hair and hat. Add mouth details and a stripe down the pant leg.

3 Complete your drawing with your felt-tip marker. Add final details and go over all pencil lines you wish to keep. Erase unwanted lines.

Caveman

1 Sketch the basic outline. Draw a long rectangle and an oval for the caveman's club.

2 Connect the shapes and round the hard edges. Draw hair and face details. Modify the legs and feet. Start adding details to the club.

3 Fill in the hair with your felt-tip marker. Draw a pattern on the caveman's clothing. Add accent lines on his ankle and elbow. Trace the pencil lines you want to keep, and erase all others.

Triceratops

1 Find out what this three-horned creature looked like. Begin by drawing some of the basic shapes, including three long ovals for the horns on its face.

2 Draw a scalloped edge on the "frill" at the back of the head. Add details to the face.

3 Use your felt-tip marker to add the final highlights and to go over the pencil marks you want to keep. Draw some detail under the feet so it looks like Triceratops is walking on land. Erase unwanted pencil lines.

Goat

Penguin

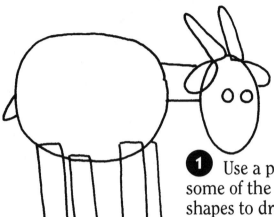

1 Use a pencil and some of the basic shapes to draw the outline. Draw two long ovals for the horns.

1 Sketch the outline lightly in pencil. Draw a rectangle on top of the head for the hat.

2 Add some details like spots on the body and legs, and a patch around one eye. Add hooves.

2 Connect the basic shapes and smooth them out to define the penguin. Add a bow tie. Refine the feet.

3 Use your felt-tip marker to fill in the penguin's arms and some of its body. Fill in the bow tie and add highlights to the hat. Go over all lines you wish to keep. Erase all others.

3 Trace over all lines you wish to keep with your felt-tip marker. Draw details on the horns and face, and fill in the hooves and the patch around the goat's eye. Erase unwanted pencil lines.

Gorilla

1 Start by drawing the basic shapes. Draw a long oval in the gorilla's left hand for his banana.

2 Soften all the hard edges to make your gorilla fluffy. Add the eye, nose, and mouth, and draw fingers and toes. Add the banana peel.

3 Make the gorilla furry by drawing short lines on his body with your felt-tip marker. Add details to the hat and to the face. Trace all the pencil lines you want to keep in your finished drawing, and erase all other lines.

Panda

1 Outline the panda using circles and ovals.

2 Connect the shapes and soften the edges. Draw the eyes, and add fingers to the hands.

3 Complete the panda by going over all the pencil lines you wish to keep with your felt-tip marker. Fill in the panda's legs, arms, ears, nose, and eye patches with your marker. Draw the mouth. Erase all unwanted pencil lines.

Dachshund

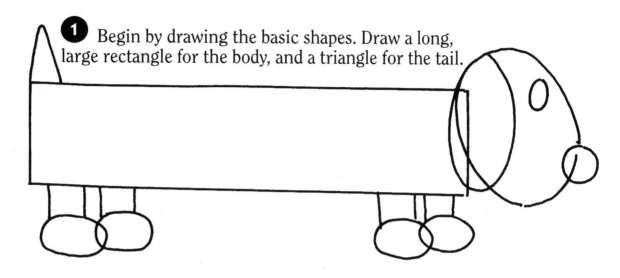

1 Begin by drawing the basic shapes. Draw a long, large rectangle for the body, and a triangle for the tail.

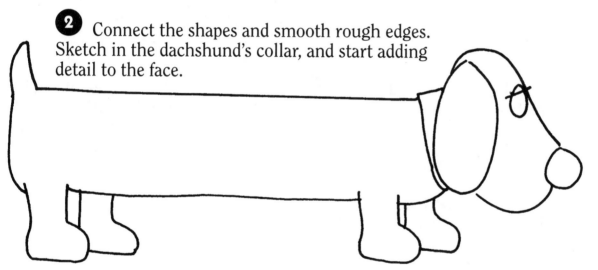

2 Connect the shapes and smooth rough edges. Sketch in the dachshund's collar, and start adding detail to the face.

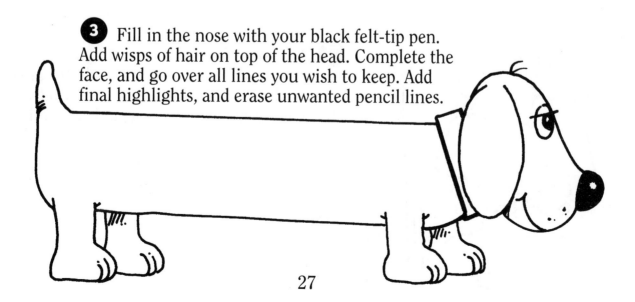

3 Fill in the nose with your black felt-tip pen. Add wisps of hair on top of the head. Complete the face, and go over all lines you wish to keep. Add final highlights, and erase unwanted pencil lines.

Viking

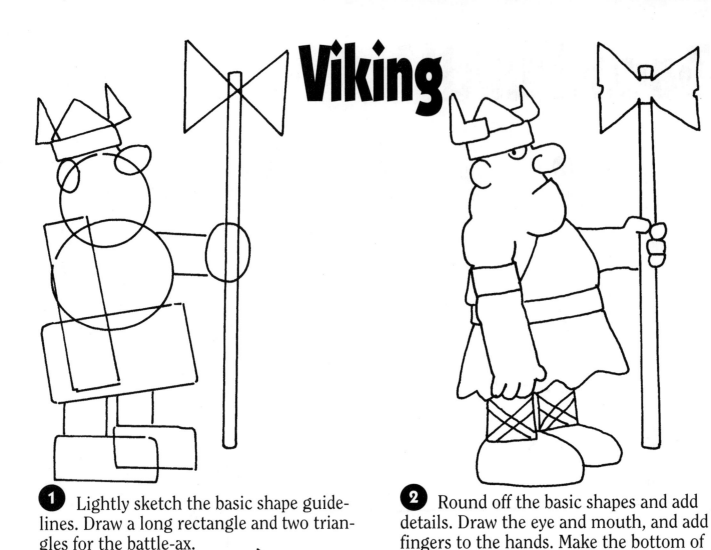

1 Lightly sketch the basic shape guidelines. Draw a long rectangle and two triangles for the battle-ax.

2 Round off the basic shapes and add details. Draw the eye and mouth, and add fingers to the hands. Make the bottom of the viking's tunic wavy. Add straps to his shoes.

3 Add some final touches with your felt-tip marker. Draw hair and a belt buckle. You may want to draw a pattern on the tunic. Go over all the lines you want to keep and erase all others.

Mountain Climber

1 Start with the basic shapes. Draw a long rectangle and two small rectangles for the pick.

2 Smooth the shapes. Draw hair and mouth. Add detail to eyes and hat. Draw the mountain climber's shorts, shirt, and suspenders. Add fingers to the hands.

3 Trace all the pencil lines you want to keep with your felt-tip marker. Draw detail on hiking boots, socks, and shirt. Add some background scenery. Erase unwanted pencil lines.

29

Kids

1 Draw the basic outline for the girl. Add a large oval and four small circles for the skateboard.

2 Smooth the edges on the shapes. Add facial details, shirt, and pants. Make the ponytail wavy at the end.

3 With your felt-tip marker add final highlights to the face, hair, and shoes. Draw fingers on hands. Add accent lines around the girl and the skateboard to give the impression that they are moving. Erase pencil lines.

1 Draw the basic outline for the boy. Add a rectangle and a large circle in one hand for the tennis racket, and a small circle in the other hand for the tennis ball.

2 Refine and smooth the basic shapes. Add eyebrows and a mouth. Draw socks and detail on the shoes. Add more details.

3 Draw hair peeking out from under the boy's cap with your felt-tip marker. Add details to the cap, tennis racket, socks, shoes, and tennis ball. Go over all the lines you want to keep and erase all others.

31

Baby

1 Begin by drawing the basic shapes. Draw a circle and a rectangle for the rattle.

2 Round the hard edges on the basic shapes. Begin adding detail to the face. Add hair and a bib. Draw fingers on the hands.

3 Use your felt-tip marker to fill in the hair. Add highlights to the bib and the rattle. Draw accent lines around the rattle so it looks like the baby is shaking it. Erase unwanted lines.